Wow, That's Woolly!

GOATS

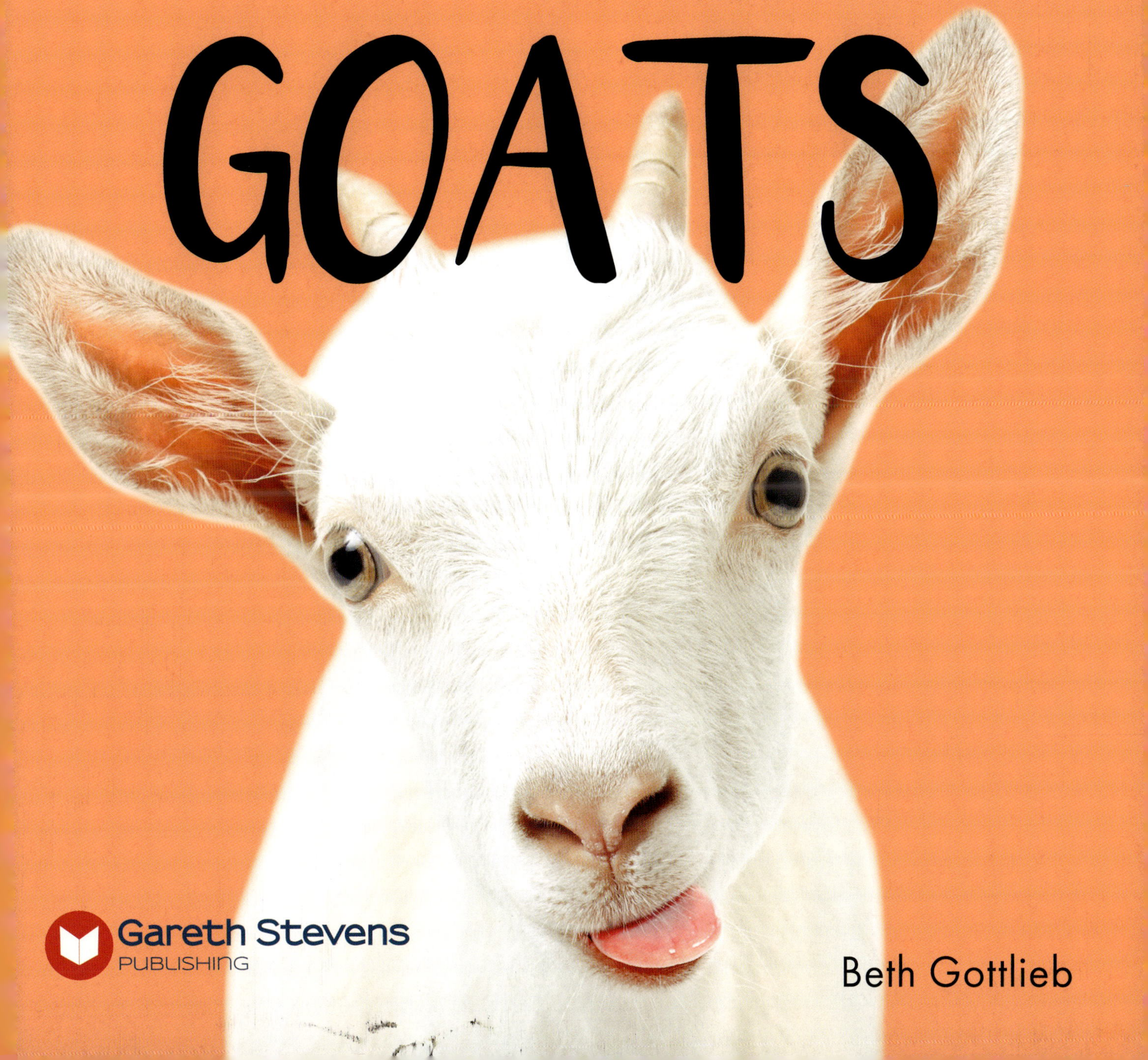

Gareth Stevens
PUBLISHING

Beth Gottlieb

Please visit our website, www.garethstevens.com. For a free color catalog of all our high-quality books, call toll free 1-800-542-2595 or fax 1-877-542-2596.

Library of Congress Cataloging-in-Publication Data
Names: Gottlieb, Beth, author.
Title: Goats / Beth Gottlieb.
Description: New York : Gareth Stevens Publishing, [2023] | Series: Wow, that's woolly! | Includes index.
Identifiers: LCCN 2021056800 (print) | LCCN 2021056801 (ebook) | ISBN 9781538279441 (set) | ISBN 9781538279458 (library binding) | ISBN 9781538279434 (paperback) | ISBN 9781538279465 (ebook)
Subjects: LCSH: Goats—Juvenile literature. | Cashmere—Juvenile literature.
Classification: LCC SF383.35 .G68 2023 (print) | LCC SF383.35 (ebook) | DDC 636.3/9—dc23/eng/20211201
LC record available at https://lccn.loc.gov/2021056800
LC ebook record available at https://lccn.loc.gov/2021056801

Published in 2023 by
Gareth Stevens Publishing
29 E. 21st Street
New York, NY 10010

Designer: Olivia Lo Sardo
Editor: Kristen Nelson

Portions of this work were originally authored by Sadie Woods and published as *Cashmere Goats*. All new material this edition authored by Beth Gottlieb.

Photo credits: Cover SonsedskaYuliia/Shutterstock.com; goat art Olzas/Shutterstock.com; p. 4 Foto2rich/Shutterstock.com; p. 5 Vera Verano Photo/Shutterstock.com; p. 6 ThaiCowboyMagazine/Shutterstock.com; p. 7 (inset) EcoPrint/Shutterstock.com; p. 7 CEW/Shutterstock.com; p. 9 David Salcedo/Shutterstock.com; p. 11 CyberKat/Shutterstock.com; p. 13 TatevosianYana/Shutterstock.com; p. 14 tuvshu.thesolidstudio/Shutterstock.com; p. 15 ChristopherWillans/Shutterstock.com; p. 17 Budmir Jevtik/Shutterstock.com; pp. 17 (inset), 19 MikhailfTurov/Shutterstock.com; p. 18 Pierre-YvesBabelon/Shutterstock.com; p. 20 Photokava/Shutterstock.com; p. 21 tomertu/Shutterstock.com

Printed in the United States of America

CPSIA compliance information: Batch #CSGS23: For further information, contact Gareth Stevens, New York, New York, at 1-800-542-2595.

CONTENTS

Woolly Goats 4
Many Kinds. 6
They Won't Eat It All!. 8
The Family Way 10
Goats and People 12
All About Mohair 14
Supersoft Cashmere 16
Shear and Spin 18
Great Goats 20
Glossary 22
For More Information 23
Index 24

Words in the glossary appear in **bold** type the first time they are used in the text.

WOOLLY GOATS

What is wool? It's any hair-like **fiber** that is produced by an animal and used to make goods for people. Sheep are known for producing the fibers used to make the **fabric** called wool. But there are many animals that have wool—including goats!

Goats have been raised by people for thousands of years. Different kinds of goats are found in different parts of the world. Almost all of them grow some kind of woolly fiber. These fibers are used to make some of the softest fabrics!

Goats may not always look soft, but some of the hairs they grow are!

MANY KINDS

There are more than 200 goat **breeds** in the world. Depending on their breed, goats can weigh anywhere from 22 to 350 pounds (10 to 159 kg). They measure between 17 and 42 inches (43 and 107 cm) tall at the shoulder.

Goats can be white, black, tan, brown, or many combinations of these colors. Often, their hair is straight, and they have a short tail. Goats can have a beard too. In addition, goats may have horns that bend backward.

PULL BACK THE WOOL

Goats have rectangular **pupils** in their eyes that can turn. This helps them keep an eye out for predators.

Boer goat

The pygmy goat is one of the smallest breeds of goat.

Angora goat

THEY WON'T EAT IT ALL!

Goats are herbivores. That means they eat only plants. Some people believe goats will eat just about anything, but this is untrue. In fact, goats are somewhat picky eaters! They enjoy leaves, sticks, stems, and grass.

Goats are ruminants, which are animals that process their food in two steps. They chew their food, swallow it, spit it back up, and chew it again. Goats have a stomach with four parts called chambers. This helps them break down their food.

PULL BACK THE WOOL

Whether wild or **domesticated**, goats are grazing animals. Grazing is moving around grassy areas eating plants.

Goats eat many plants that people think of as weeds!

THE FAMILY WAY

Goats are **mammals**. They live in herds, or groups. Goat herds usually have a female leader called a herd queen. A male goat is called a buck or a billy. A female goat is called a doe or a nanny. Young goats are called kids.

Mother goats often have two kids at a time. Kids can stand as soon as they're born and are able to walk within a few minutes of being born. Their mothers care for them when they are young.

PULL BACK THE WOOL

Goats reach adulthood when they're about a year old. On average, they live for about 12 years. Some live even longer.

Every goat has its own call and **scent**. Mothers use their kids' scents to find them.

GOATS AND PEOPLE

Goats are friendly creatures. They are easy to keep on a farm. Goats were some of the first animals to be domesticated by people. Goats may have been the first animals people kept for milk. They have also been used to pull carts and carry packs. Goatskin was once used to make parchment, or paper, to write on and bottles to carry liquids.

Today, people continue to keep goats for their milk, meat, and wool.

PULL BACK THE WOOL

Goat milk can be made into cheese and yogurt!

Goats can be very friendly. Most like being petted and played with.

ALL ABOUT MOHAIR

There are two main kinds of fibers produced by goats: mohair and cashmere. Angora goats produce mohair. Some Angora goats have hair that grows in ringlets, and others have hair that is flat, which looks wavy. Mohair is a long, smooth fiber. It's strong and has **luster**.

Angora goats are commonly **sheared** two times a year. Angora goats that live on farms in the United States may produce more than 5 pounds (2.2 kg) of mohair each time they are sheared!

PULL BACK THE WOOL

The fiber known as angora doesn't come from Angora goats. It is produced by Angora rabbits.

The United States, Turkey, and South Africa produce the most mohair in the world.

SUPERSOFT CASHMERE

Cashmere goats aren't an actual goat breed. The name "cashmere goat" can be used to describe any goat that produces cashmere wool. Cashmere comes from the supersoft undercoat of goats.

Cashmere goats can be sheared once a year. One goat produces as much as 2.5 pounds (1.1 kg) of **fleece** per year. Only a small part of this fleece is cashmere. Some farmers may choose to comb or pluck the fiber from their goats rather than shear them.

PULL BACK THE WOOL

A micron is a unit by which hair or fiber is measured. Cashmere fiber must be 19 microns or smaller. That's very thin compared with human hair and other animal fibers.

Today, most cashmere goats are the **descendants** of meat and dairy goats that were bred because of the high amount of cashmere fiber they produced.

cashmere fibers

SHEAR AND SPIN

Once a goat is sheared, the outer guard hair is removed from the fibers that are collected. This is called dehairing. Machines often do large-scale fiber processing. However, many people work their fiber at home.

After it's sorted and cleaned, fiber can be spun. Spinning is the process by which fiber is made into yarn. The longest, thinnest pieces of fiber are used for knitted cloth. The shorter fibers are used for cloth made by weaving.

PULL BACK THE WOOL

Historically, cashmere was the cloth greatly liked by royalty and wealthy people.

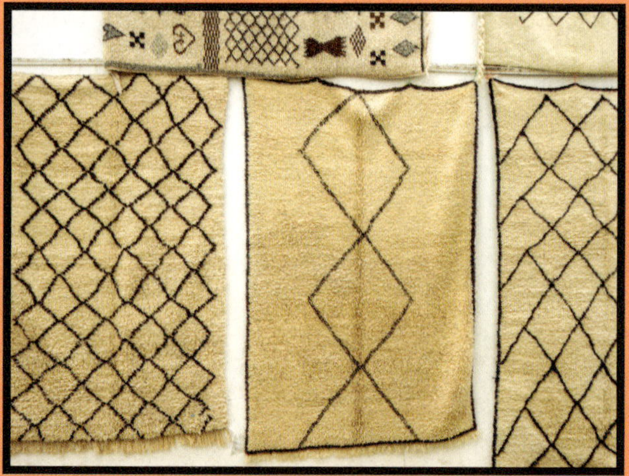

mohair rugs

Goats' guard hairs can be used for rugs. Both mohair and cashmere are used to make clothing.

GREAT GOATS

Cashmere is one of the softest **materials** in the world. Raising cashmere goats has just begun to grow in **popularity** in the United States. Most of the world's cashmere is produced in China, Afghanistan, Iran, and India.

Both mohair and cashmere have been used to make goods for people for thousands of years! These soft fibers are very popular today and can cost a lot of money. It's amazing that they come from a well-known farm animal—the goat!

PULL BACK THE WOOL

Cashmere wool is sometimes called pashmina.

The earliest recorded use of cashmere was back in the 14th century. Mohair is thought to have been used even before that!

GLOSSARY

breed: A group of animals that share features different from other groups of the same kind.

descendant: An animal that comes from an animal of an earlier time.

domesticated: Bred and raised for use by people.

fabric: A kind of cloth.

fiber: A thin thread of natural or human-made material that can be used to make cloth.

fleece: An animal's wool coat.

luster: The glow created by reflected light.

mammal: A warm-blooded animal that has a backbone and hair, breathes air, and feeds milk to its young.

material: Matter from which something is made.

popularity: Having to do with being liked by many people.

pupil: The black part in the center of an eye that lets in light.

scent: A smell.

shear: To remove the hair or wool from.

FOR MORE INFORMATION

Books

Brinker, Spencer. *Baby Goats.* Minneapolis, MN: Bearport Publishing, 2021.

Culliford, Amy. *Goats.* New York, NY: Crabtree Publishing, 2021.

Websites

Easy Science for Kids: Goat Facts

easyscienceforkids.com/best-goats-in-a-tree-video-for-kids/

Check out some quick facts about goats here.

Find Out! Goats

www.dkfindout.com/us/animals-and-nature/domesticated-animals/goats/

Read more about goats and other domesticated animals.

Publisher's note to educators and parents: Our editors have carefully reviewed these websites to ensure that they are suitable for students. Many websites change frequently, however, and we cannot guarantee that a site's future contents will continue to meet our high standards of quality and educational value. Be advised that students should be closely supervised whenever they access the internet.

INDEX

Angora goats, 7, 14
beard, 6
billy, 10
Boer goat, 6
breeds, 6, 7, 16
buck, 10
cashmere, 14, 16, 17, 18, 19, 20, 21
cashmere goats, 16, 17, 20
color, 6
dehairing, 18
doe, 10
eyes, 6
food/what they eat, 8, 9
grazing, 8
hair, 4, 5, 6, 14, 16, 18, 19
height, 6
herd queen, 10
herds, 10
horns, 6
kids, 10, 11
microns, 16
milk, 12
mohair, 14, 15, 18, 19, 20, 21
nanny, 10
pashmina, 20
pupils, 6
pygmy goat, 7
ruminants, 8
scent, 11
shearing, 14, 16, 18
sheep, 4
spinning, 18
stomach, 8
tail, 6
weight, 6
wool, 4, 12, 16, 20